Believers But Strangers In the Eye's of God

Believers
But
Strangers
In the Eye's of God

Discovering how professed believers can still be strangers in the Eye's of God

Sharon D. Meadows

Copyright © 2007 by Sharon D. Meadows.

ISBN: Hardcover   978-1-4257-9774-4
         Softcover   978-1-4257-9769-0

All rights reserved. No part of this book may be reproduced or transmitted in any form or by any means, electronic or mechanical, including photocopying, recording, or by any information storage and retrieval system, without permission in writing from the copyright owner.

This book was printed in the United States of America.

copyright reg number:txu945-959
web address:www.sharondmeadows.com
email address: heavenlyangel@bellsouth.net

To order additional copies of this book, contact:
Xlibris Corporation
1-888-795-4274
www.Xlibris.com
Orders@Xlibris.com

Contents

Introduction	Christianity Undercover	11
Chapter 1	"The Unknown You"	13
Chapter 2	Strangers to God, but Friends to the Enemy	19
Chapter 3	Killing the Esau Inside!	24
Chapter 4	"I Want God to Know my Name"	29
Chapter 5	How to Mend the Broken Fellowship?	35
Chapter 6	Sincerity of Your Belief	40
Conclusion	Living Truth to What You Believe	47
Section II	Inspirational Poems for the Soul	49

I credit this message to God the Father, the Son, and the Holy Spirit. I'm privilege to be called as your servant and mortal mouthpiece. You are truly the inspiration behind this book! I thank you for giving me the strength and diligence to complete this assignment. You believed in me and predestined this time to be. I honor you with obedience and with the best of my abilities. "Just have your way." "For you called, I answered, and was chosen to be blessed!"

"So Glory be to you God, my father, my friend, forever more!"

Special Acknowledgments

My family, my friends, forever will I adore.

To my armor bearers who believed in my God-given talent, it was you who encouraged me every step of my journey. With gratitude, I thank you and appreciate your kindness. It's nice to know true love, which is a gift from divinity. Its qualities are rare and only a few will find it. Priceless in value, even the rich couldn't own it! I'm blessed to experience its passion and delight in its presence with you.

Introduction

Christianity Undercover

Christianity has become a mockery of the twenty-first century. Our faith has been ridiculed, rejected, and examined suspiciously. Our divine experiences are discredited as mediocre and make-believe. We have been arrested and held as captives to this world. Our names have been labeled to minimize our credibility, and most of all, our existence is being threatened due to lack of unity. Why have we become prisoners of our faith? And why have we allowed Satan to intervene this way?

Many of us have camouflaged our identities. We have compromised ourselves to gain the acceptance of others. Blinded by the pleasures of this world, we trade in eternity for temporary forms of gratification. We have lost our distinction and divine uniqueness. Our actions have dishonored the most "High God" and have placed us in position for suspension.

Saints, we've become friends with the enemy! He erased our memory and gave us amnesia. Most of us don't know who we are and the power that we possess. Although we portray to be believers of God, we are mere strangers in bondage to this world. Our spiritual ignorance has qualified us to be candidates of Satan's deception. Presently, we are confused in thinking our actions are acceptable, and no matter what the consequences we're unconcerned beyond today.

As true Christians, we have an obligation to be more! Our lives should be reflective of God's words. Instead of being hypocrites, our walk should be filled with spirit and great truth. Imposters are eventually exposed and denied their place within eternity. The decision is ours to make. Do we walk in defeat or regain our authority? Divine power is in our change. Let's discover our destiny and walk in God's purpose accordingly.

"My prayers are with you on this journey!"

Chapter 1

The Unknown You

Make every effort to enter through the narrow door, because many, I tell you, will try to enter and will not be able to. Once the owner of the house gets up and closes the door, you will stand outside knocking and pleading, "Sir, open the door for us." But he will answer, "I don't know you or where do you come from." Then you will say, "We ate and drank with you, and you taught in our streets." But he will reply, "I don't know you or where you come from. Away from me, all you evil doers!"

—Luke 13:24-27

What if a stranger knocked on your door this instant? Would you invite him in for tea, cookies, and a friendly conversation? Or would you say, "Who are you?" and "What do you want?" If you were the least bit sane and somewhat competent, you would not invite a stranger into your home. To protect the safety of your family and yourself, you should avoid becoming a statistic of today's brutality. Interrogation should be done through the door, while promptly dialing the police for help! What you do in the next few seconds is vital in securing your existence. The thought of such a situation is frightening when your safety is in jeopardy, and the outcome could be fatal!

This is a description of "the unknown you." God is saying, "Who are you?" and "What do you want?" To clarify further, let's explore Matthew 22:1-8.

> Jesus spoke to them again in parables, saying: "The kingdom of heaven is like a king who prepared a wedding banquet for

his son. He sent his servants to those who had been invited to the banquet to tell them to come, but they refused to come. Then he sent some more servants and said, "Tell those who have been invited that I have prepared my dinner. My oxen, and fattened cattle have been butchered, and everything is ready. Come to the wedding banquet." But they paid no attention and went off—one to his field, another to his business. The rest seized his servants, mistreated them and killed them. The king was enraged. He sent his army and destroyed those murderers and burned their city. Then he said to his servants, "The wedding banquet is ready, but those I invited did not deserve to come."

Imagine we have just been invited into the kingdom. God has prepared such awesome things that our eyes have not seen. The invitation has specially arrived with an RSVP needed. We looked at it, opened it, and rejected it. Our earthly circumstances have made us too busy to attend. We have prior obligations, business commitments, leaving us with no spare time to go. In the end, guess what? God rejects us too! (Proverbs 1:22-33).

Our heavenly seats are taken and given to those deserving of them. We've been labeled strangers in the eyes of God and his kingdom. Our actions have deviated against his will and separated us from his presence.

Jesus said, "Many are called, but only a few are chosen." It's true! Although we've received the invitation, we deny it by our daily actions. We would rather be hearers but not doers, talkers but not walkers, professors but literally hypocrites to the faith. What does God have to say about us? Listen carefully to the words of James:

> Do not merely listen to the word, and so deceive yourselves. Do what it says. Anyone who listens to the word but does not do what it says is like a man who looks at his face in the mirror and, after looking at himself, goes away and immediately forgets what he looks like. But the man who looks intently into the perfect law that gives freedom, and continues to do this, not forgetting what he has heard, but doing it—he will be blessed in what he does. (James 1: 22-25)

Acknowledging "The Unknown You"

Not long ago, I was an "unknown you." I would attend church regularly to praise, pray, and pretend. Although I was a stranger to God majority of the week, I became his best friend on Sunday morning. I would shout so loud my voice would become hoarse. I was a spiritual fake and a deceiver to myself. The Gospel says, "If we claim to have fellowship with him yet walk in darkness, we lie and do not live by the truth" (1 John 1:6).

I never considered myself in darkness. I was a believer of God, an active churchgoer, and an open professor always expressing love toward the Gospel, yet I was an alien to it. My actions were merely traditional, with no genuine individual experience. I was in direct error to God's will and walking in dead authority.

To prevent my soul from perishing, I needed a wake-up call. My spirit began craving for more. I wanted to experience the fullness of God's presence, but didn't know how. Spending time with him was essential, and the best place to begin was the book. The book that would give me identity and reveal knowledge to the whole world today is the Holy Bible.

Saints, we all should be fed daily from the word of God. It's the only food that can satisfy our hunger and thirst in life. Nothing tangible can take its place because our fulfillment comes from our indulgence in Christ. If we are willing to consume, he'll suppress and fulfill our appetites.

In order to regain our direction in life, we must seek truth. Viewing ourselves transparent is vital for change. The law is a mirror image, and our ways are being reflected and revealed. We can look beyond our flaws and pretend of no existence, or make the necessary corrections. Our exposure is obvious, but why do we constantly deny our errors?

Recognizing the Enemy's Schemes

Satan has truly hardened the hearts of many. He has successfully made us apathetic in our emotions. Most have no interest in being sincere and would rather remain pretenders until exposed. As a result, our souls are being ransomed to pay for his pleasures. We've become puppets of his amusement and, with continued participation, have altered our future destination.

> The sinful mind is hostile to God. It does not submit to God's law, nor can it do so. (Romans 8:7)

> The eye is the lamp of the body. If your eyes are good, your whole body will be full of light. But if your eyes are bad, your whole body will be full of darkness. If then the light within you is darkness, how great is that darkness! (Matthew 6:22-23)

The enemy's ultimate strategy is to inhabit your mind and blind your sight! Once this mission is complete, your actions can be predicted, determined, and controlled. His goals have been achieved in the *past* and will be accomplished in the *future*. The tactics used are clever and seducing even to the most intelligent. If he can control what you think, eventually he will control you! Consequently, you'll remain blind to your purpose and destiny. You may never fulfill the assignment God chose you to do on earth.

Satan also preys upon the family. He desires to conquer the head knowing the body will be automatically awarded. Spiritually, the head of the family is the husband and the body consists of the wife and children (1 Corinthians 11:3). When Satan controls the head, he disconnects the union and brings forth chaos. The wife becomes frustrated, the kids lack self-control, and the husband becomes a robot of his destruction. What can one do when peace is destroyed in the home?

I believe, if we surrender to the headship of Jesus Christ, our families can be restored and our wounds can be healed.

It Happened in the Past

The Pharisees were deceived by Satan's schemes. Although they were biblically educated and intellectual teachers, they were ignorant to the Son of God. Jesus described them as "teachers of the blind" and "spiritual hypocrites" (Matthew 23). He prophesied in the last days that those that are blind would see, and those that see will become blind (John 9:39).

This is truly a great description of the Pharisees. They were double-minded and didn't practice what they preached. They were no different than you or I, who act as pagans. The resemblance is similar, and some of our thoughts and actions are identical. Jesus exposed them (and us) perfectly when saying, "You hypocrites! Isaiah was right when he prophesied about you: 'These people honor me with their lips, but their hearts are far from me. They worship me in vain; their teachings are but rules taught by men'" (Matthew 15:7-9).

It is God's will for all of creation to enter his kingdom. The choice is ours, and the power rests in our individual free will. We were born with an option to do good or to do evil. Knowing the difference between right and wrong elevates us to a level of accountability. In the end, we can either be accepted or rejected, but what we do today will ultimately determine our fate.

The worst error we can make is to labor our whole life in vain! We can imitate the Pharisees in their destruction or prevail to a plateau of excellence. The shocking mystery I find in people is their ignorance of not knowing what they do. They feel innocent regarding their actions and seem clueless about their behavior. Even though they have not repented or changed, they look forward to being welcomed into eternity. Their deception derives from the myth that there are no consequences for our earthly actions. They seek to gain their reward in this life and the one to come. Does this sound familiar to you? Or do you know someone who resembles this description?

It's Happening Today

Not everyone who says to me, "Lord, Lord," will enter the kingdom of heaven, but only he who does the will of my Father who is in heaven. Many will say to me on that day, "Lord, Lord, did we not prophesy in your name, and in your name drive out demons and perform many miracles?" Then I will tell them plainly, "I never knew you. Away from me, you evildoers!"

—Matthew 7:21-23

Satan, who is the *"God of this world,"* has blinded the eyes of many (2 Corinthians 4:4). He has planted deception in the hearts and minds of those willing to live in darkness. The problem arises when we can't identify his plan or our own spiritual blindness.

Presently, we live life as usual and never plan our future. We desire to fulfill our pleasures no matter the expense. We often take time for granted and assume to live another day. Delaying our change is the master trick of the enemy. If he can get us complacent, his work will be complete.

Today, God is warning us repeatedly. He's showing *all* mercy before he disciplines. The time is now! And this message I proclaim to everyone. Another day is not promised, or even another breath beyond our breathing (James 4:13-17). What are we so afraid to give up? And why do our knees tremble at the thought of change? If we reject God's will today, he'll reject our will tomorrow.

Regaining spiritual sight is a necessary defense. If we continue our journey with no vision, we will miss our purpose in life. Destiny can be aborted and wasted time will leave us broken in spirit. Ultimately, we can remain blind or mimic the men who requested healing to see (Matthew 20:29-34). The decision is ours, but we must use wisdom when making it.

"The unknown you" has become a battlefield for Satan. He has used this weapon to literally destroy us! We must regain our memory then put on our heavenly armor (Ephesians 6:11). It's our only defense to stand against the enemy. The war has begun, and we're all scheduled for battle. Before taking our positions, let us begin to pray.

> Heavenly Father, we come boldly to your throne for mercy and grace. We pray that your ears are attentive to our confession and request for change. Please forgive "the unknown you" and pardon our lack of fellowship and spiritual ignorance. Turn every heart back to you for purification and edification. Bring forth new minds with new thoughts of you. Destroy the chains of darkness that hold many of us in bondage and teach us how to do your will. We cast down any hosts of evil that come against this plea and pray that everyone will walk in the fullness of life the way you intended. We ask it all and believe it's done.
>
> In Jesus's name, Amen.

Chapter 2

Strangers to God but Friends to the Enemy

And there was war in heaven. Michael and his angels fought against the dragon, and the dragon and his angels fought back. But he was not strong enough, and they lost their place in heaven. The great dragon was hurled down—the ancient serpent called the devil, or Satan, who leads the whole world astray. He was hurled to earth, and his angels with him. Therefore rejoice, you heavens and you who dwell in them! But woe to the earth and the sea, because the devil has gone down to you! He is filled with fury, because he knows that his time is short.

—Revelation 12: 7-9,12

What if I told you the god you serve is really your enemy? The one you adore and worship truly hates you. Would you believe me or declare me insane? Or would you be wise and listen carefully to what I say? The evidence is shocking, and the information revealed may save your soul!

> So I say, live by the Spirit, and you will not gratify the desires of the sinful nature. For the sinful nature desires what is contrary to the Spirit, and the Spirit what is contrary to the sinful nature. They are in conflict with each other, so that you do not do what you want. But if you are led by the Spirit, you are not under the law. The acts of the sinful nature are obvious: sexual immorality, impurity, and debauchery; idolatry and witchcraft; hatred, discord, jealously, fits of rage, selfish ambition, dissension, factions and envy; drunkenness, orgies, and the like. I warn you, as

> I did before, that those who live like this will not inherit the kingdom of God. (Galatians 5:16-21)

If these scriptures exposed some skeletons in you, then it's obvious—you've been serving the wrong god! The one who blinded your sight and taken you as captives, we call him Satan (2 Corinthians 4:4; 1 John 5:19). His name varies throughout history, but his motives remain the same. His mission is to *kill, steal,* and *destroy.* He is the author of confusion, the father of all lies, and the adversary to God's creation. Why would you become friends with the enemy? And why involve yourself into his eternal destruction? Is it because you truly believe you're covered under spiritual immunity? Well, let me reveal some truth to your misunderstanding.

> Do you not know that the wicked will not inherit the kingdom of God? Do not be deceived; neither the sexually immoral, nor idolaters, nor adulterers nor male prostitutes, nor homosexual offenders, nor thieves, nor the greedy, nor drunkards, nor slanderers, nor swindlers, will inherit the kingdom of God. And that is what some of you were. But you were washed, you were sanctified, you were justified in the name of the Lord Jesus Christ and by the Spirit of our God. (1 Corinthians 6:9-11)

The key word in the above scripture is *were.* If you notice, this word is used in past tense and not the present. If you are presently participating in any of these offenses, you need to seek God today for deliverance! There is no reason for Christians to live in bondage daily. Jesus came to give us life and life more abundantly (John 10:10). Committing these sinful acts brings death, the very opposite of his plan.

Not long ago, I cancelled my friendship with the world of Satan. I decided to be true to the faith that I professed. There was only one problem—I needed to *die!* (Romans 12:1). I had to kill the old life full of sin. Getting rid of my will and honoring God's will was challenging, but I had to do it. My soul depended upon it!

Initially, the task was difficult. It was as if Satan entered my mind as soon as I committed to change. He became my shadow and eagerly enticed me for a season. He offered presents that were captivating, but when examined they were volatile, filthy, and corrupt. His strategy was to get me off focus. If he could accomplish this, I would no longer be a threat to his mission. Beyond my greatest carnal desire, I resisted his temptations. I began discerning and fleeing from his clever schemes. I had made a covenant with God and wasn't about to dishonor it for the enemy.

Rejecting the Adversary to Serve God

"What good will it be for a man if he gains the whole world, yet forfeits his soul? Or what can a man give in exchange for his soul?" (Matthew 16:26). This is the question we should ask. *What*, or *who*, is hindering our purpose in life? Is it material goods that die beyond this world? (Timothy 6:7). Or is it our self-will that's too stubborn to change?

I am not a psychic, but can only see what God has allowed me to discern. I believe the reason Christians lack spiritual growth is due to immaturity in the faith. We fail to excel and bear fruit representing our salvation (1 Peter 2:2-3). This limited advancement can be blamed on our uncommitted hearts. We are too afraid to give God total control. The truth of the matter is, he already has it!

Constantly, we battle with our spirit to preserve our flesh, and consequently end up weary, tired, and frustrated. We were never created to operate beyond the parameters of God. We were given power to conquer our flesh but have failed to exercise it appropriately. As a result, we're being controlled by the nature we were given authority over. We have chosen the world over God and his kingdom. We would rather serve them both, but our actions would never be justifiable. A severing of ties from this world is needed to gain access to his glory. If we refuse to change, then how can we be eligible to reap the rewards?

It's amazing how we truly expect something for nothing. We pursue great blessings from little praise and worship. When we pray at night, we anticipate an answer the next morning. It's like dining at your finest restaurant without paying the bill, or filling up your gas tank and then driving away. How can you expect a harvest when no seeds have been planted? You have to give in order to receive, and forsake in order to gain. No one could say it better than the apostle James, who boldly expressed this statement:

> You want something but you don't get it. You kill and covet, but you cannot have what you want. You quarrel and fight. You do not have, because you do not ask God. When you ask, you do not receive; because you ask with wrong motives, that you may spend what you get on your pleasures. You adulterous people, don't you know that friendship with the world is hatred toward God? Anyone who chooses to be a friend of the world becomes an enemy of God. (James 4:2-4)

We must retaliate against Satan and expose his plan. Our goal should be to separate from his worldly system. We should live as aliens or strangers to anything unlike God, and nothing should be exalted above his will (1 Peter 1:17). Our kingdom is not of this world, and our present existence is temporary. We are foreigners without a permanent visa, here on assignment with purpose and destination. Our citizenship is heaven bound and conditional to our actions on earth. This world should not be a priority. We should be strangers to it and from anything that war against our souls! (1 Peter 2:11-12).

Regaining Friendship with a Friend

Greater love has no one than this that he lay down his life for his friends. You are my friends if you do what I command. I no longer call you servants, because a servant does not know his master's business. Instead, I have called you friends, for everything that I learned from my Father I have made known to you.

—John 15:13-15

Many of us don't know what true friendship is. We practice it to the limitations of our carnal abilities. Some may think they have it, but when the storms of life come, they end up deserted, devastated, and deceived. What is the definition of a true friend? And who is qualified to show love unconditionally? "For God so loved the world that he gave his one and only son, that whoever believes in him shall not perish but have eternal life" (John 3:16).

What an awesome sacrifice! Do you know anyone who would give his or her life to save yours? If there is the slightest doubt inside your mind, the answer is probably not.

True friendship is rare, and only those who sincerely know God can share it with you. I testify to my own experiences after tasting the fruit of its bitterness.

A few years ago, the poison of friendship bit me. I was destroyed when every friend I had was exposed. They were wolves in sheep's clothing and portrayed themselves lovely (Matthew 7:15). I thought they cared for and truly loved me, but every ounce of their efforts were conditional. The relationships were superficial, and time revealed this all.

For years I was blind and very ignorant. I failed to see them as acquaintances or maybe even companions, but they were not my true friends. The Gospel says, A friend loves at all times, and a brother is born for adversity (Proverbs 17:17).

The Gospel also says, A man of many companions may come to ruin, but there is a friend who sticks closer than a brother (Proverbs 18:24).

Most of my friendships were failures. I trusted more in flesh than in spirit and spent more time with them than with God. I had forsaken my *first love* and neglected his company. I was blind to the enemy's scheme of separation. Amnesia was his weapon, but my memory began to fight back! I started thinking about what Jesus did for me. If anyone had been a traitor to friendship, it was I. I had become friends with the adversary and actively participated in his world. Godly sorrow pierced my heart, and I began to cry. I needed to confess my misdeeds and ask for his forgiveness.

My concept was totally wrong! I thought people could make me complete. Our bodies were never designed to be fulfilled by flesh because we're spiritual beings created by God. He is the only one who can fill our void. There is no one on earth who can replace his presence or mimic his authenticity. If we try to substitute, our plan will fail and leave us incomplete. Depression will enter and deplete the joy we have. So what can we do to prevent these consequences? And how can we regain friendship with a friend?

I believe we can start by trusting our Lord. Jesus said, "But seek first his kingdom and his righteousness, and all these things will be given to you" (Matthew 6:33). Do you believe him? If so, you can start by serving him today!

Chapter 3

Killing the Esau Inside!

What is an Esau, and who can be one? is the question you may be asking? The answer is clear and may be quite shocking as you explore this vital chapter.

An Esau is one who thrives on immediate gratifications in life, who lives for today with no hope, cares, or concerns for tomorrow. It is one who takes pride in obtaining worldly wealth to promote an image, or to finance earthly pleasures. It can be a friend, brother, sister, or even yourself.

The life of an Esau is ruled by flesh and not governed by the Spirit. It has a "right now" attitude and demands everything upon request. Its immature spirituality is primarily caused by the lack of patience. An Esau wants it "today," and tomorrow isn't good enough. It is one who loves the world and has given it permission to possess its soul.

Mentality of an Esau

Once when Jacob was cooking some stew, Esau came in from the open country, famished. He said to Jacob, "Quick, let me have some of that red stew! I'm famished!" Jacob replied, "First sell me your birthright." "Look, I'm about to die," Esau said. "What good is the birthright to me?" But Jacob said, "Swear to me first." So he swore an oath to him, selling his birthright to Jacob. Then Jacob gave Esau some bread and some lentil stew. He ate and drank, and then got up and left. So Esau despised his birthright.

—Genesis 25:27-34

"Quick, fast, and hurry" is the motto of an Esau. No matter what the cost, they want it right now! This was the attitude the twin of Jacob had. He sold his future for a better today. Instead of planning his hunt precisely, he ran out of time and eventually suffered greatly. His carelessness paved the way to get rejected by God, his father, and eventually himself. An Esau lived inside and influenced his mistakes. He was conquered by it, was controlled by it, and ultimately was led astray. Discovering his purpose was never fulfilled because his destiny had been altered. He remained barren and lived life less than he intended.

Not long ago, an Esau controlled my life. I remember fighting with my flesh and losing the battle vividly. I wanted a new car and began looking one Saturday morning. A sports car was ideal, something that was fast, attractive, and extremely fashionable.

It was one hot summer morning. I wanted to look good and at the same time keep cool. My mother and I arrived at the dealer, and there in front of me was the "apple of my eye". It was clean, shiny, and waiting just for me. Besides, it had my name written all over! The salesman came up, and I inquired about this car. He gave me the keys; I smiled and opened the door. I sat down quickly, relaxed in its cushions, and gazed at the leather dash. My eyes opened in surprise when I discovered the mileage and cost of the vehicle. I felt nauseous and my stomach began turning like a carnival Ferris wheel. I didn't know what to do and desperately needed some help.

My Esau came quickly to the rescue. It told me how good I looked in this car, and the color was truly perfect for me. It never said anything about the future mechanics of the car. Its comments were superficial and catered only to my flesh. What was I to do? This question plagued my mind. The salesman came up, and I asked him to negotiate a better deal. He smiled and replied, "If I reduce it any more, you'll be buying the car for free." My palms became sweaty, and my heart pounded faster. It was up to me to make the final decision.

Before I could say yes, my spirit conquered my flesh and told me no. I obeyed, cancelled the deal, and moved forward. Relieved by the decision I made, I rushed into the restroom to pause. I was disappointed, but knew I had done the right thing. Instantly, I had a vision like never before. I saw a new green sports car beside me. In my hand were the keys and several important papers. I could see my face and the emotions of my happiness. Finally, I had the car I wanted to enjoy. God was showing me the future of something more. He was going to bless me, but today was not the season. I dried my eyes, adjusted my posture, and left the showroom. Although I didn't have the car, I was pregnant with a vision. For once in my life I was sure of something I couldn't see, called *faith*.

Consequences of an Esau

Esau said to his father, "Do you have only one blessing, my father? Bless me too, my father!" Then Esau wept aloud. His father Isaac answered him, "Your dwelling will be away from the earth's richness, away from the dew of heaven above. You will live by the sword and you will serve your brother. But when you grow restless, you will throw his yoke from off your neck."

—Genesis 27: 38-40

Esau's name is not biblically known, but his actions labeled him as flesh. He was rejected by God, was branded with a father's curse, and was exiled to a place called Edom. This land was mostly desert and useless for cultivation. Located south of the Dead Sea, it was the home of Esau. He was a hunter who enjoyed the wild, and now lived among the wilderness. Today, how many of us reside on this dry land?

Presently, there are many Esaus around. You can find them in disguise or open to their carnal preferences. They are people who lack self-control and demand everything instantly! They often accuse God of being too slow and taking too long to bless. As a result, they hire flesh and terminate the job of the Spirit. They become godless and dependent upon themselves. In the end, they lose faith and get discouraged with living life (Galatians 6:9).

Saints, if we walk in obedience to the Holy Spirit, he will subdue our flesh. God never intended for it to rule over our lives. He ordained us to conquer and discipline its nature. Our obligation is to stay in communion with Christ and prevent flesh from separating us from his presence.

Killing the Esau Inside!

In the same way, count yourselves dead to sin but alive to God in Christ Jesus. Therefore do not let sin reign in your mortal body so that you obey its evil desires. Do not offer the parts of your body to sin, as instruments of wickedness, but rather offer yourselves to God, as those who have been brought from death to life; and offer the parts of your body to him as instruments of righteousness. For sin shall not be your master, because you are not under law, but under grace. What then? Shall we sin because we are not under law but under grace? By no means!

—Romans 6:11-15

I believe most of us are not walking in the spirit. We live by our sinful nature and become offenders of the law. When exploiting our lives this way, we nullify the purpose and mission of Christ. Our passions and worldly pleasures are yet to be crucified. Saints, this should not be! Our spirit must govern our daily operations. It should control who we are and take precedence over our nature. There should be no hesitation toward change, but faith along with total submission. So why do we constantly violate God's will? And why do we often cater more to our flesh?

The enemy has done an excellent job in warping our minds. Our perception of life has been unrealistic and disturbing. The whole world has advertised to Satan's corruption, and many of us are guilty of buying it! We practice what the majority do and become unified with his worldly indiscretions. The Gospel says, "Do not be deceived: God cannot be mocked. A man reaps what he sows. The one who sows to please his sinful nature, from that nature will reap destruction; the one who sows to please the spirit, from the spirit will reap eternal life" (Galatians 6:7-8).

In the past, I dated guys who catered more to my flesh. They were pleasing to the eye but spiritually wrong for my life. I would often wonder how someone who looked so good could be so bad for me. This was a constant struggle within my spirit. I wanted to operate in flesh and enjoy its pleasures today. Adopting this rebellious attitude caused me lots of pain, agony, and distress. My heart was broken in two, and relationship baggage became my burden. Although I knew the truth, I suppressed it to do what I wanted. For many years, my life was unproductive to God's will.

Throughout biblical history, an Esau controlled many mighty men of God. They allowed fleshly desires to be exalted above their spirit. As a result, kingdoms, rulers, and empires came to a ruin. Many were rejected after denying the warnings of God. They were blinded by the tricks of the enemy and proved the joke was on them!

Isn't it easier to live for today and forsake tomorrow? Yes, but the consequences are inevitable! You cannot expect life when your actions birth death. You cannot be resurrected until you've been buried with Christ. This misconception has allowed Satan to gain control. He has deceived many and disguised his tactics cleverly. We must accept truth and acknowledge needed change. It's our only weapon against his defense. Let us regain our spirit and listen to its voice internally. "Obedience is a necessary virtue for our survival."

Chapter 4

"I Want God to Know my Name"

A name is something given to recognize identity. It can be short, long, simple, or complicated in speech. Its primary purpose is to reveal one person to another. Over the years, it may acquire a reputation similar or contrary to the world. "A good name is more desirable than great riches" (Proverbs 22:1). It can be an excellent source in promoting your image, or a destroyer of life itself. Unfortunately, a bad name is like a shadow. It follows you wherever you go.

I often remember the names of persons and places. If the experiences were positive, I would continue to associate, but if they were negative, I would terminate all contacts completely. It's like canceling a debt before it comes to haunt you, or removing yourself before a negative situation explodes.

One concept I vividly remember is that most people get offended when you forget their name. If you remember it, watch their faces light up like Christmas trees. A sense of importance is what people want to feel, and it's you or I who gives it to them.

Before our parents named us, I believe they planned it with great intentions. They desired a good name that would be respected and honored. We were given that name to positively represent us instead of negatively tainting our character. Today, we should adopt this same attitude. We need to be proud of who we are and strive for excellence. Our goal should not be to discredit or to hurt our image, but to enhance it by preserving our name.

A Stranger has no Authority in Hell

God did extraordinary miracles through Paul, so that even handkerchiefs and aprons that had touched him were taken to the sick, and their illnesses were cured and the evil spirits left them. Some Jews who went around driving out evil spirits tried to invoke the name of the Lord Jesus over those who were demon-possessed. They would say, "In the name of Jesus, whom Paul preaches, I command you to come out." Seven sons of Sceva, a Jewish chief priest, were doing this. One day the evil spirit answered them, "Jesus I know, and I know about Paul, but who are you?" Then the man who had the evil spirit jumped on them and overpowered them all. He gave them such a beating that they ran out of the house naked and bleeding.

—Acts 19:11-16

When God knows your name all of hell knows it too. They are trembling with fear because of the power you possess. You can now walk in authority and command for demons to "come out!" They must recognize your voice because God has anointed you and demanded their obedience. He has honored your name and presented you as commander in chief. There is nothing on earth or in hell to stop you. Once God has given you the power, all of creation has to submit.

What an awesome Lord we serve! If we make ourselves committed, can we obtain this power? Certainly yes! All we have to do is be faithful to the God we serve. We must honor and revere him to gain access to his glory. Once access is granted, all of hell will acknowledge our name.

God Knew Them by Name

When you are in right relationship with Christ, you are no longer a goat of this world, but a sheep of the kingdom. Jesus said, "My sheep listens to my voice. I know them, and they follow me" (John 10:27). You will flee from a stranger's voice, but recognize the voice of God (John 10:3-5).

How many of us can honestly hear his voice? I believe very few, due to our lack of fellowship. In the past, the minority was able to hear. Although they were few in number, they were distinguished among millions. Three examples of those who heard and harkened to the voice of God were Moses, Job, and Samuel. They were called into destiny by name and one was privileged to be called by God face-to-face.

The Call of Moses

Now Moses was tending the flock of Jethro his father-in-law, the priest of Midian, and he led the flock to the far side of the desert and came to Horeb, the mountain of God. There the angel of the Lord appeared to him in flames of fire from within a bush. Moses saw that though the bush was on fire it did not burn up. So Moses thought, "I will go over to see this strange sight—why the bush does not burn up." When the Lord saw that he had gone to look, God called to him from within the bush, "Moses! Moses!" And Moses said, "Here I am."

—Exodus 3:1-4

Can you imagine being called this way? The thought may be inconceivable and, at the same time, quite scary! The Lord knew Moses face-to-face and gave him power to perform many miracles. He was also known as "the humblest man in all the earth," who found favor in the eyes of God (Numbers 12:3). Moses can be credited for many things. He led the Israelites out of Egypt, inscribed the Ten Commandments, and was a visionary to the promised land of Canaan. Although he was slow in speech, Moses was a model representative for God's people. Today, he is a pioneer of the Bible and should be remembered and honored by all. His death was premature, which caused much grief among the Israelite community. "Since then, no prophet has risen in Israel like Moses, whom the Lord knew face to face who did all those miraculous signs and wonders in the land of Egypt" (Deuteronomy 34:10-11).

The Call of Job

One day the angels came to present themselves before the Lord, and Satan also came with them. The Lord said to Satan, "Where have you come from?" Satan answered the Lord, "From roaming through the earth and going back and forth in it." Then the Lord said to Satan, "Have you considered my servant Job? There is no one on earth like him; he is blameless and upright, a man who fears God and shuns evil. "Does Job fear God for nothing?" Satan replied.

—Job 1:6-9

Not only did God know Job's name, but Satan knew it as well. Job's perfections elevated him to a level of great honor. Although he was tested repeatedly, he remained pure and upright in his ways. In the end, he was redeemed from his troubles and restored to his rightful place. Job was tempted beyond our imagination, but God was faithful and didn't burden him beyond his fortitude. His wife and friends thought he was crazy and encouraged him to curse the will of God. Job refused and became a laughingstock of his town. His love for God was greater than any person or anything, and he would die before he renounced his faith or abandoned our Lord.

How many of us would give up everything for God? Would we trust him and believe in his timely deliverance? Could we remain faithful even though our names are being ridiculed? Most probably we wouldn't. We've become predictable in our dealings with earthly situations. When trouble arises, we fail to view it as only temporary. Our circumstance becomes overwhelming and entices us to compromise. Eventually, we drop out of the race and grow weary. It's because we've forgotten who we are and the power that we possess. Satan has taken our memory, and we have failed to regain it!

Job never got amnesia. He always knew who he was and the Lord of all creation. Although he grieved often, he didn't confuse it with God's hatred for him. He was aware of his love and remained hopeful in his redemption. Job knew if the Lord was willing, he was surely able. He wanted to live, but only as one who had been faithful to the Almighty God.

The Call of Samuel

One night Eli, whose eyes were becoming so weak that he could barely see, was lying down in his usual place. The lamp of God had not gone out, and Samuel was lying down in the temple of the Lord, where the ark of God was. Then the Lord called Samuel. Samuel answered, "Here I am." And he ran to

Eli and said, "Here I am; you called me." But Eli said, "I did not call; go back and lie down." So he went and lay down. Again the Lord called, "Samuel!" And Samuel got up and went to Eli and said, "Here I am; you called me." "My son," Eli said, "I did not call; go back and lie down." Now Samuel did not yet know the Lord: The word of the Lord had not yet been revealed to him. The Lord called Samuel a third time, and Samuel got up and went to Eli and said, "Here I am; you called me." Then Eli realized that the Lord was calling the boy. So Eli told Samuel, "Go and lie down, and if he calls you say, 'Speak, Lord, for your servant is listening.'" So Samuel went to lie down in his place. The Lord came and stood there, calling as the other times, "Samuel! Samuel!" Then Samuel said, "Speak, for your servant is listening."

—1 Samuel 3:2-10

Before he was conceived in his mother's womb, Samuel was called to serve God. After birth, he was given unto the Lord to honor a vow made by his mother. She promised that if God would allow her to conceive, she would give him her first son. When Samuel was only an infant, she fulfilled that promise. She gave him to Eli, the priest, to minister before the Lord. As Samuel grew in age, God's favor grew with him. He became known as a just man in heaven and on earth.

How many of us would love to be recognized? I suspect everyone would. The thought of God acknowledging you is greater than anything you could think of.

I remember in grade school when we had Honor's Day. This was a day when all students who had excelled would be rewarded. I lived for this event, and when it came I anxiously waited for them to call my name. When the teacher reached the podium, my heart raced and my palms became sweaty. Impatiently, I waited to hear her remarks. When she finally spoke and her lips uttered my name, I leaped like a frog! Excited to receive my award, I shook her hand and danced back to my seat. It felt good. It's like winning a million-dollar lottery She only recognized my name, and that was truly enough honors for me.

Listening for the Call of Your Name

If God called your name this minute or this second, would you be able to hear his voice? Could you hear him speak in your present situation? Or would you be qualified or disqualified from the call? I believe many would miss his voice. Due to our hectic routines, there is little time left to hear. We've become preoccupied and lost within the world. Instead of being alert and in position, we are unprepared for anything. We have unified ourselves with the norm and evolved into objects subject to wrath.

Why have we deviated from his will? And why have we grown deaf to the voice of God?

Saints, we are guilty of being too busy! We spend more time in the natural than in the spiritual realm. As a result, we become drained, empty, and routinely depressed. We've exerted too much energy and received nothing. We were never designed to function this way. In order to be complete, we need God to assist us. Devoting intimate time to him prepares us to hear his voice, but we must quiet ourselves and eliminate every distraction. Who knows? "God may be calling your precious name!"

Chapter 5

How to Mend the Broken Fellowship?

My mother once said, "How can you fix something when you can't see it's broken?" Or, "How can the blind be a leader over those who see?" This is the question I ask, how can you change when you don't see the necessity for changing?

The answer is extremely difficult to conceive, because most Christians have lost sight of what they were supposed to see. They believe their barren situation is normal or common, but fail to see the truth within. Somehow, Satan has deceived many, and this deception has caused death and separation from God. He has purposely thrown us off focus to hinder the fulfillment of our assignments. We've become puppets of his production and led astray by false hopes of stardom. How has he done this? you may be wondering. It's shocking! He has done this in front of our eyes and we have failed to detect it!

Indulging in Worldly Fellowship

What is Worldly? Acting in an unholy manner, which causes one to deviate from the will and authority of God.

What fellowship can light have with darkness? This question I ask with Paul (2 Corinthians 6:14). Many of us are guilty of limited communion with God and have chosen the world to do most of our affiliations. We indulge in all sorts of detestable idolatry and claim to be sold out to Christ. Our membership with the Church of Laodicea has aroused great jealously in God. He has watched our waywardness and in anger issued judgment on us all!

> I know your deeds, that you are neither cold nor hot. I wish you were either one or the other! So, because you are lukewarm, neither hot nor cold, I am about to spit you out of my mouth. You say, "I am rich; I have acquired wealth and do not need a thing." But you do not realize that you are wretched, pitiful, poor, blind and naked. (Revelation 3:15-17)

In the past, I was guilty of this betrayal. I loved the Lord, but desired the world and its pleasures. Instead of giving up either of them, I actively participated in both. My relationship with God was meaningless if I couldn't offer a sacrifice of change. Jesus Christ did when he died on the cross to fulfill his earthly purpose. He did it to restore life and not to minimize it by our sins. It's the opposite of God's will for us to live unfruitful lives. We are supposed to be productive and prosperous people. If we obey, then our obedience will be rewarded, but if we rebel, it could cost our very souls!

> For I do not want you to be ignorant of the fact, brothers, that our forefathers were all under the cloud and that they all passed through the sea. They were all baptized into Moses in the cloud and in the sea. They all ate the same spiritual food and drank the same spiritual drink; for they drank from the spiritual rock that accompanied them, and that rock was Christ. Nevertheless, God was not pleased with most of them; their bodies were scattered over the desert. Now these things occurred as examples to keep us from setting our hearts on evil things as they did. Do not be idolaters, as some of them were; as it is written: "The people sat down to eat and drink and got up to indulge in pagan revelry." We should not commit sexual immorality, as some of them did; and in one day, twenty-three thousand of them died. We should not test the Lord, as some of them did, and were killed by the destroying angel. These things happened to them as examples and were written down as warnings for us, on whom the fulfillment of the ages has come. So, if you think you are standing firm, be careful that you don't fall! (1 Corinthians 10:1-12)

Many of us have fallen and failed to get up. We wallow in misery and self-pity to make excuses for our actions. We feel justified in blaming Satan for our repeated mistakes, but it's our choice to resist his temptations. God has given us all the gift of free will. Freedom to choose is wonderful, but it must be exercised appropriately. We can seek divine help and be governed by our spirit, or controlled by our flesh within. The option is given to be defeated or victorious over the enemy. Today is our opportunity to decide, but if we claim to know God, our relationship must represent him in truth.

Making Room for Private Communion

When Jesus was only a boy, he knew the importance of private time with God. He would often disappear from people to be alone to pray. Once when he was very young, he accompanied his parents in travel. They would annually attend the Feast of the Passover in Jerusalem. After the event, his parents returned home, but Jesus stayed behind in the temple. He would sit among the teachers, listening to them and asking questions to their amazement. When his parents discovered his disappearance, they returned to Jerusalem anxious and filled with grief. When they arrived Jesus asked, "Why did you seek me? Did you not know that I must be about My Father's business?" (Luke 2:49). How many of us can honestly say we have? I assume the majority has been about themselves instead of taking care of business for God.

Living out of communion with Christ is like playing an instrument out of tune. You cannot get the correct notes unless you practice it routinely. In time, the sounds played will produce melodies of sweet music. Our worship should mimic this perception. Every Christian must prioritize communion with God. We need this time to gain power against the enemy. In order to repel his deadly arrows, we must wear our spiritual defense. "For our struggle is not against flesh and blood, but against the rulers, against the authorities, against the powers of the dark world and against the spiritual forces of evil in the heavenly realms" (Ephesians 6:12).

Getting to know Jesus Christ is like getting to know *yourself*. Over time, he'll reveal who you are and what purpose God has for your life. Mysteries and secrets will be uncovered to provide knowledge needed on your journey. No longer will confusion flood your mind, but clarity will reside to give you peace. In the end, God is faithful in granting the desires of your heart. If you remain loyal, he'll fulfill your every need. How is this done? you may be wondering. It's simple, but you must honor the commitment to serve him first!

Making room for private communion is equivalent to making room to eat. When prioritizing this, you'll receive strength from the spiritual food consumed. It doesn't take much to communicate to the Almighty God. He can hear you *anywhere, anytime,* or *anyplace.* He is ready on all occasions to listen and to speak, but you must be in position to receive. If you're not, you could miss his voice and lose your sense of direction. Ultimately, you would fail the test and never reach the next level. This immaturity would leave you unfit to benefit God's kingdom on earth.

Understanding Corporate Fellowship

And let us consider one another in order to stir up love and good works, not forsaking the assembling of ourselves together, as is the manner of some, but exhorting one another, and so much more as you see the Day approaching.

—Hebrew 10:24-25

Isn't it wonderful to wake up on Sunday morning and go to church? We arise early to get dressed in our nice clothes and shoes previously picked the night before. Our face is well washed, hair is nicely groomed, and we are advertising our favorite fragrances. Can you imagine getting dressed this way before entering God's house of prayer? This image is what many of us portray as we duplicate this weekly pattern.

I believe it is God's will for us to assemble corporately. To praise and worship on one accord brings forth power. Reaching saints through the Gospel, the angel of the house gives hope, direction, and clarity in life. He prays and intercedes on God's judgment to allow us another chance. Even though his efforts are done earnestly, the outcome may be unsuccessful. If our hearts are hardened and resistant to change, the word will never penetrate our spirit. "We will be ever seeing but never perceiving and hearing but never understanding" (Matthew 13:14). In time, we'll grow frustrated and question the validity of God. Forbidden doubt will invade our mind, leaving us skeptical of every good work.

Saints, when we are together corporately, our pastor should not have to labor. The word of God preached should only be a confirmation. Its origin should begin with *you*, instead of being birthed from the pulpit. If we are not exercising this freedom, we are truly going to war without armor. We will lose and be defeated every time. Due to our inexperience and absence of faith, we are unfit and unskilled for battle. The word of God will never become our reality because we're unwilling to live within it. We use it out of convenience or to enhance our image, but never trust and believe in its power.

My Lord, please forgive us! And welcome this prayer to your glorious throne.

> Heavenly Father, Have mercy on our uncommitted hearts. We confess to our lack of fellowship and communion with you. We promise in the future to be better stewards representing your kingdom. Forsaking not the intimate time requested by you, but seeking your presence at all times. We acknowledge our misdeeds; therefore, we ask for your forgiveness and grace to help us change. Teach us how to trust in you! We submit unto your perfect plan and honor your divine will. Pour mercy upon us all!
>
> In Jesus's name, Amen.

CHAPTER 6

Sincerity of Your Belief

Jesus declared, "Believe me, woman, a time is coming when you will worship the Father neither on this mountain nor in Jerusalem. You Samaritans worship what you do not know; we worship what we do know, for salvation is from the Jews. Yet a time is coming and has now come when the true worshipers will worship the Father in spirit and truth, for they are the kind of worshipers the Father seeks. God is spirit, and his worshipers must worship in spirit and in truth."

—*John 4:21-24*

Have you ever heard the phrase "The truth shall set you free," or "What you do in the dark will come to the marvelous light"? Coincidently, both of these phrases are true according to the living words of the Almighty God (John 8:32; Ephesians 5:13).

I remember clearly suppressing the truth throughout my teenage years. I would often lie about my age to feel and look more mature. One lie led to another, and eventually I became this fictitious person. No longer could I live as me, but I had to be another who was make-believe. My disguise would last for a season, but the truth would finally expose it all. When the time came and everything unraveled in the light, I felt embarrassed, ashamed, and miserable about my dishonesty. As a result, my date abandoned me and my credibility was ruined. No longer was I known by my native name but was labeled and classified as a liar.

Saints, "*imposters* of the Gospel" should not be our image!

We should strive to be honest and live righteous lives. If we are to be chosen in the end, our worship must be filled with spirit and truth. Our Heavenly Father looks for this sincerity and will not accept anything less. He requires perseverance, pure works, and obedience toward him. *"Therefore if anyone is in Christ, he is a new creation; the old has gone; the new has come!" (2 Corinthians 5:17)*. We must discipline our lives to meet the requirements and expectations of God. Our change is the only way to enter into his kingdom.

Maturing in Our Salvation

If you are convinced that you are a guide for the blind, a light for those who are in the dark, an instructor of the foolish, a teacher of infants, because you have in the law the embodiment of knowledge and truth—you, then, who teach others, do you not teach yourself? You who preach against stealing, do you steal? You who say that people should not commit adultery, do you commit adultery? You who abhor idols, do you rob temples? You who brag about the law, do you dishonor God by breaking the law? As it is written: "God's name is blasphemed among the Gentiles because of you."

—Romans 2:19-24

When I became a true believer of the faith, I was shocked by the actions of my brothers and sisters in Christ. My heart grieved with sorrow, and my eyes cried tears out of disbelief. I could not fathom how some of the profound professors of Christianity could become traitors. Enemies of God by what they portrayed in their daily lives. How could saints, who have once been enlightened, get entangled back in the world? Of them the proverbs are true: "'A dog returns to his own vomit,' and 'a sow, having washed, to her wallowing in the mud'" (2 Peter 2:22).

Over two thousand years ago, Jesus predicted this event. He prophesied that many would grow weary and turn away from doing good. He knew the perfect priest would become the dark angel of hell. There are many today and tomorrow who will make the transformation. They will choose the path of destruction and forsake the narrow way of life.

I never implied that worshiping God *in truth* would be easy. It takes diligence and compliance to succeed. There will be adversities and massive tribulations, but our adoption is on the way! (Romans 8:14-16). If we remain hopeful, we'll qualify for the kingdom and rule a thousand years with Christ. So why do many forsake the way of the true and living God? They grow impatient with what they cannot see.

The Lord of our salvation is clearly testing our faith. He's keeping a record of those who fear, honor, and revere his name (Malachi 3:16). Our ways are being recorded, our conversations are being heard, and our actions are being scrutinized very closely. Our duty is to preoccupy and take care of business, instead of becoming idle robots of Satan's workmanship. We should be expanding our territory and allowing the blessings to flow on earth as they are in heaven.

Overtime, we've become complacent with our present situation. We have lost the desire to accomplish and achieve more. We settle for "whatever" and become content with our failures. This unfruitful attitude has allowed the enemy to gain control. When he rules, he devours our total zeal for God. We develop a slacker's attitude and get comfortable with our salvation. As a result, we fall into sin and make excuses for our actions. We become repeat offenders and abuse the spirit of grace. I believe many of us will die in the wilderness. We will never discover our destiny, and all efforts done will be in vain!

Christians' Hypocrisy

You may be wondering how you can stay pure in a world so corrupt. Or how God's commands can be honored when temptation entices you daily. To be honest, it cannot be done alone. You need divine help, and that assistance comes from above.

> How can a young man keep his way pure? By living according to your word.
>
> Seek you with all my heart; do not let me stray from your commands.
>
> I have hidden your word in my heart that I might not sin against you.
>
> Praise be to you, O Lord; teach me your decrees.
>
> With my lips I recount all the laws that come from your mouth.
>
> I rejoice in following your statutes as one rejoices in great riches.
>
> I meditate on your precepts and consider your ways.
>
> I delight in your decrees; I will not neglect your word.
> (Psalms 119:9-16)

Saints, through Jesus Christ, we are more than conquerors (Romans 8:37)! There is nothing on earth or in hell to prohibit our Lord. If you are a born-again Christian, Jesus lives within you. He'll provide the power you need to overthrow the enemy. Satan and his demons will have to flee from the anointing that rests upon you.

God has given us authority since the beginning of time. We *all* have either the ability to change or remain engaged in our evil desires. The problem arises when we try to participate in both. Jesus said, "No one can serve two masters. Either he will hate the one and love the other, or he will be devoted to the one and despise the other" (Matthew 6:24).

Saints, we cannot be sheep during the day and wolves at night, or angels on Sunday and hell-raisers during the week. There is a major difference in knowing the word and actually living it! Presently, we should be examples of Christ in the flesh. If we choose not to be, then we can blame ourselves in the end.

It's sorrowful to say that most of us are walking vessels of judgment. Our present existence is contingent upon our obedience. So why do we gamble each day not knowing what the next may bring? The answer is a mystery yet to be solved. We consistently live life as a treat and overindulge in its sweetness. Over time, we get sick of all the problems we've encountered. We complain and argue, but continue to satisfy our appetites. One day *you* must decide to "choose this day whom you will serve" (Joshua 24:14). If your choice is proper, you could avoid God's wrath on the disobedient.

The Lord shows love to those who keep his decrees, but hatred toward those who violate them. Our actions alone can either release or hold us in bondage. We must stop blaming Satan for our misdeeds and assume responsibility. It is God who gives us free will and it's our choice to apply it righteously. If we don't comply, we are dead already according to biblical truths (Ephesians 2:1-2).

A Purpose to be Fulfilled

Therefore, since Christ suffered in his body, arm yourselves also with the same attitude, because he who has suffered in the body is done with sin. As a result, he does not live the rest of his earthly life for evil human desires, but rather for the will of God. For you have spent enough time in the past doing what pagans choose to do—living in debauchery, lust, drunkenness, orgies, carousing and detestable idolatry. They think it's strange that you do not plunge with them into the same flood of dissipation, and they heap abuse on you. But they will have to give account to him who is ready to judge the living and the dead.

—1 Peter 4:1-5

Have you ever wondered why you are here and what purpose God has for your life? Did you know we all have an individual assignment to complete? For many years, I was ignorant regarding my existence. I thought the American dream was to get married, have children, and be successful financially. Consequently, I was wrong! My vision disabled me to see. This was the world's dream instead of God's will for me.

I believe Christ desires for us to be pioneers of our purpose. We should be seeking or walking boldly in our destiny. Each day, living is a blessing to maneuver us in the right direction. We should not be headed backward but moving forward in the things of God. It may take persistent prayers and intimate communion to reveal his divine plan, but it is our spiritual duty to pursue it!

If you already know your earthly purpose, then you must be fulfilling it daily. Presently, you should be maturing and developing in your gifts. You should know *who you are* and what God has assigned you to do. Your obedience to his call expresses true commitment and your mission is to carry on the work he has ordained.

Many of us quote biblical scriptures, but do we clearly understand their meaning? And if we do, do we apply faith when reciting them from our mouth? One famous proverb to all is Romans 8:28. It reads, *"And we know that in all things God works for the good of those who love him, who have been called according to his purpose."* We repeatedly misinterpret its meaning. Our true understanding is in the two. Yes, God will work for the good of those who love him, *but* they must be called according to his purpose. You cannot expect assistance when you're out of order to God's will. He truly adores you but helps those who help themselves. He is an awesome Lord who requires your total submission. If you sincerely seek your purpose, he will reveal his plan. Your footsteps will be ordered to precisely complete your assignment.

Another duty to our mission is to minister the word to each other. Before Jesus ascended to heaven, he gave this final command, *"Go and make disciples of all nations, baptizing them in the name of the Father and of the Son and the Holy Spirit, and teaching them to obey everything I commanded you"* (Matthew 28:19-20). Saints, we are supposed to be snatching people from the fire instead of burning with them (Jude 1:22)! Our goal should be to witness, but we are falling into the very sin we are witnessing about. My brothers and sisters, this should not be! We must become believers who worship in truth. Instead of being living hypocrites, we should be imitators of God. Our mentality and image should be of the righteousness within. The spiritual success we desire is contingent upon our obedience, and until we are poured out like a drink offering, our mission is yet complete! (2 Timothy 4:6).

I challenge you today to explore and discover your destiny. Seeking God's plan and purpose for your life is imperative! Your divine gifts and talents should be utilized for his kingdom and not contaminated with this world. Your heavenly goal is to be all that God has ordained you to be. As a reward, he will offer you eternity, giving you a place to dwell with Christ forever. There is nothing on earth or in hell worth forfeiting this privilege. Your soul is what the enemy desires and he will do *whatever* to possess it! Even though his power is influential, his efforts are limited to your free will. The choice is yours to either accept or reject his ways. If you decide to enter the narrow path of righteousness, peace and blessings will overtake you. A doorway into your destiny will open, and the Holy Spirit will govern your purpose. *"Let your gifts be known throughout the land!"*

Conclusion

Living Truth to What You Believe

Discovering "true believers" have become difficult in a world comprised of *strangers*. The lack of spiritual sincerity has invaded the hearts of many, making the task impossible to fulfill. Searching for diamonds and precious jewels in haystacks full of thorns can be extremely exhausting. If we desire to become representatives of Christ, our behavior must portray his salvation. We can no longer participate in subtle disobedient practices but must be true to the faith we proclaim. Imposters have no place in the kingdom and will find residence in the fires of everlasting hell. So why do we gamble every moment on earthly pleasures when the end could be seconds away? Is it because we abuse the love of God when taking his grace in vain?

Today is our opportunity to change! The commitment to become righteous is overdue and outdated for many. It takes obedience to surrender, and I pray that I will influence your submission. The Lord foreknew if this message would be accepted or rejected, but it was still my assignment to complete it. I hope the words from this book will pierce your spirit and remodel your heart. There should be no doubt but faith in all the things God ordained.

It's amazing how people will believe worldly rumors but contradict biblical truths. I never could fathom the reason why. My heart shows compassion toward their spiritual ignorance but fear of the road they may encounter. Will it be heaven or hell, life or death, acceptance or rejection from God?

When seeking our destiny, life's hardships will cause weariness, "but those who wait on the Lord shall renew their strength; they shall mount up with wings like eagles, they shall run and not be weary, they shall walk and not faint" (Isaiah 40:31). God is a faithful guide through every temptation, but we must be willing to endure. Acquiring patience and perseverance will prepare us for the task and give us hope in his timely redemption. There is a race that everyone must run and a test that must be completed by all. In order to reach the next level, our achievements must be satisfactory. We should all be groomed and decorated like soldiers of war to conquer the enemy. When the battle is over and our loyalty remains, we will hear our father's voice saying, *"**Well done, my good and faithful servant. Come and take your place inside my kingdom!**"*

Inspirational Poems for the Soul

I present these heart-filled poems as a token of my adoration. To you I share these words to encourage and strengthen your spirit. May they open your mind and minister change to your thoughts. I hope the seeds planted will produce a harvest, and I declare every heart will be obedient to receive. May your soul be blessed by the affirmations from my spirit, and may you offer them to others on their journey. Remember, "be joyful always; pray continually; give thanks in all circumstances, for this is God's will for you in Christ Jesus" (1 Thessalonians 5:16-18).

Inspirational Poems for the Soul

I	*Faith*	53
II	*Whispering*	54
III	*Alone No More*	55
IV	*How Can You Love Me?*	56
V	*If I Should Stay?*	57
VI	*Prince Charm*	58
VII	*Why I Hope?*	59
VIII	**Love**	60

Faith

What is this thing people call faith?
You can't see it, touch it, smell it, or taste it.
It's invisible to the natural eyes
It lives within and dwells deep inside.
You need a little of it to start each day
And be your defense to shield the evil away.
What is this thing people call faith?
That's impossible for any man to make!
Its power is strong and never ever too weak
When the season comes this little faith shall speak.
Boldly with force but showing some love
Fulfilling every promise given it from above.
Why can't you find it in any running fountain?
And how on earth could this faith move mountains?
It's unique and original in style.
If you feed it some hope, it'll grow up like a child.
Why do we all need this precious little gem?
Because without it, it's impossible to please him!

Whispering

I hear whispers all around
They travel like lightning before hitting the ground.
The impact is great when it hits my mind
The damage is recorded in a matter of time.
They try to possess and try to control
They may even try to build up strongholds.
They disguise themselves cleverly from me
But I'm not deceived, they are my enemies.
I hear them everywhere, yet I'm not alarmed
For I am equipped, they can do me no harm.
"Listen carefully, don't you hear?
They're trying to enter, but I have no fear."
I pick up my shield, which is my faith
And the Holy Spirit will lead the way.
The word of God will be my sword
To fight this battle and gain my reward.
The struggle is over and I have won
Yet my journey is still undone.
I still hear them even though I've been crowned
There will always be whispering around!

Alone No More

Who am I? And where do I belong?

It's crazy here, inside me, all alone.

I wonder what did I do so wrong

To cause such emptiness inside my home.

I see darkness in this place

There is no light within my space.

No happiness, No joy, No laughter, No noise

Just empty, "Oh, God, I feel guilty!"

I drop down to my knees, I confess, and I plead

"Oh, Jesus, my Lord, won't you help me!"

"Be Quiet! I just heard a knock

Or is it my heartbeat about to stop?"

I heard it again so I dried my eyes

And opened my heart in great surprise.

It was Jesus coming into me

He promised that he would always love me.

He held me tight and dried my tears

I felt safe and free from fear.

The light came in and the darkness went away

I'm happy to say it was a brand new day!

How Can You Love Me?

How can you love me the way that you do?

I have done nothing but disappoint you.

I have been selfish right from the start

But you chose to dwell inside my heart.

Why am I so special to you?

Why not move out for a day or two?

You could roam freely throughout this world

And never return to this old girl.

There are many willing to worship you

With all their hearts because they love you.

Why do you stay when I misbehave?

And why forgive me when I bow down and pray?

Wait a second; I've got a clue!

I think I know why you do what you do.

Many years ago you died on the cross

To save my life so I wouldn't be lost.

If I can believe what you did this day

You promised to help me every step of the way.

I can do nothing to make you flee

I've just accepted you would always love me!

If I Should Stay

Should I stay? Or should I go?

This is the question I already know.

Inside my heart I still deny

What will it take for me to realize?

What is the true reason I can't see?

Why am I blind to this strong hold on me?

Inside, I feel so much pain

If I should stay there will be no gain.

My spirit says *yes,* but my flesh says *no*

Where on earth would I be able to go?

If I should stay I'll do nothing but cry

And live in misery until I die.

The war inside is more than I can take

I need some help before I break.

Why am I blind? Why can't I see?

"Is there anybody out there listening to me?"

Who can guide me and take my hand?

I've found my answer, *Jesus* can!

Prince Charming

One day soon I will be complete
And filled with joy from this man I'll meet.
Clothed in splendor, his love is tender
His chivalry is so attractive to me.
A smile that is sexy, his manners well-behaved
When I look in his eyes he puts me in a daze.
What did I do to deserve all this?
I keep asking myself, "Girl, is this really it?"
Got to be a fairy tale or maybe even a dream
This is the best thing that ever happened to me!
As I start to panic, he reaches out for my arm
And takes me down the isle to be my forever
PRINCE CHARM!

Why I Hope?

You ask me why I have the hope that I do
When my world is crumbling down in two.
Why do I laugh when I should be sad?
I JUST SMILE AND LOOK AT YOU.
Why do I keep moving along?
Why am I singing a happy praise song?
Why do I behave the way that I do,
When there are so many struggles I'm going through.
I JUST SMILE AND LOOK AT YOU.
Why do I continue to preach and teach?
Why am I always in perfect peace?
Why aren't I weeping and crying?
I should quit and end this trying
I JUST SMILE AND LOOK AT YOU.
AND . . .
I say, "Come here, dear, the answer is clear.
When you're in the storm you know Jesus is near.
To lead the way his power is unstoppable.
Just remember through him, all things are possible!"
THIS IS THE REASON I HOPE.

Love

Love is the greatest gift from above
It's bigger than anything you can think of.
Love is the ability to show compassion
Regardless of words, it will be your action.
Love is forgiving anyone's mistakes
It's right on time and never ever too late.
Love is respectful, peaceful, and kind
It dwells in your heart and lives in your mind.
Love is attraction, or a magical potion
It's crazy sometimes and full of emotion.
Love is cute and sometimes odd
But most of all, ***love is God!***

IS THIS YOUR LOVE?

GOD, WE DID IT!

Printed in the United States
109356LV00005B/412-420/A